T0287300

URBAN VANS

PERPETUAL CALENDAR

"A VAN FOR EVERY DAY"

The instagram page

@vansofberlin

is collecting vans, trucks and camping vans in all variations on the urban streets since 2014.

instagram.com/vansofberlin

Volkswagen LT Hightop Camper

1
JAN

Volkswagen Type 2 / T3 Hightop Camper

vansofberlin.com

2

JAN

Mercedes-Benz 710 4WD Expedition Truck
vansofberlin.com

3
JAN

Mercedes-Benz 307 D Arnold Camper
vansofberlin.com

4
JAN

Ford Transit MK1

vansofberlin.com

5

JAN

Mercedes-Benz Alkoven Camper

vansofberlin.com

6

JAN

Volkswagen Type 2 / T3 Dehler Profi Hightop Camper
vansofberlin.com

7
JAN

Itasca Winnebago RV Motorhome
vansofberlin.com

8
JAN

MAN 415 DIESEL 4WD Expedition Mobile
vansofberlin.com

9
JAN

Volkswagen Type 2 / T3 Poptop Camper

vansofberlin.com

10
JAN

Mercedes-Benz 508 D Camper Van
vansofberlin.com

11
JAN

Mercedes-Benz 608 D Hightop Camper
vansofberlin.com

12
JAN

Volkswagen Type 2 / T3 Poptop Camper
vansofberlin.com

13
JAN

Mercedes 207 Camper
vansofberlin.com

14
JAN

Mercedes-Benz 207 D Hightop Camper
vansofberlin.com

15
JAN

Toyota Hiace / Arca Pfeil II Alkoven Camper

vansofberlin.com

16
JAN

Barkas B 1000
vansofberlin.com

17
JAN

Mercedes-Benz 613 D Camper

vansofberlin.com

18

JAN

Volkswagen Type 2 / T3 Poptop Camper
vansofberlin.com

19
JAN

Volkswagen Type 2 / T3 Syncro Hightop Camper
vansofberlin.com

20
JAN

Ford Transit MK2
vansofberlin.com

21
JAN

Mercedes-Benz 813 Custom Camper Truck
vansofberlin.com

22
JAN

Mercedes-Benz 609
vansofberlin.com

23
JAN

Volkswagen LT Alkoven Camper
vansofberlin.com

24
JAN

Volkswagen Type 2 / T3 Doka
vansofberlin.com

25
JAN

Mercedes-Benz 508 D Custom Camper
vansofberlin.com

26
JAN

Volkswagen Type 2 / T1
vansofberlin.com

27
JAN

Mercedes-Benz 308 Hymer-Mobil 700
vansofberlin.com

28
JAN

Büssing DE65 Event Bus
vansofberlin.com

29
JAN

Volkswagen Type 2 / T3 Poptop Camper
vansofberlin.com

30
JAN

Mercedes-Benz O 309 Camper
vansofberlin.com

31
JAN

Opel (Bedford) Blitz Hymer-Mobil 521 Camper

1
FEB

Subaru Libero E12 Super Deluxe 4WD

vansofberlin.com

2

FEB

Volkswagen Type 2 / T3 Transporter
vansofberlin.com

3
FEB

Volkswagen Type 2 / T3 Hightop Camper
vansofberlin.com

4
FEB

Opel (Bedford) Blitz Hymer-Mobil 521 Camper

vansofberlin.com

5
FEB

Ford Transit MK2 Pilote
vansofberlin.com

6
FEB

Volkswagen Type 2 / T3 Transporter Camper
vansofberlin.com

7
FEB

Volkswagen Type 2 / T3 Hightop Camper
vansofberlin.com

8
FEB

Volkswagen Type 2 / T3 Pemamobil Hightop Camper

vansofberlin.com

9

FEB

Mercedes-Benz Hymer-Mobil 540 Camper
vansofberlin.com

10
FEB

Steyr 680M 4WD Expedition Truck

vansofberlin.com

11

FEB

Volkswagen LT Hightop Camper
vansofberlin.com

12
FEB

Volkswagen Type 2 / T3 Joker Hightop Camper
vansofberlin.com

13
FEB

Mitsubishi L300 Alkoven Camper

vansofberlin.com

14
FEB

Volkswagen Type 2 / T2 Camper
vansofberlin.com

15
FEB

Ural 6WD Expedition Truck

vansofberlin.com

16
FEB

Volkswagen Type 2 / T3 Hightop Camper

vansofberlin.com

17

FEB

Ford Transit MK2
vansofberlin.com

18
FEB

Volkswagen LT 35 Niesmann + Bischoff Clou Alkoven Camper
vansofberlin.com

19
FEB

Volkswagen Type 2 / T3 Hightop Camper
vansofberlin.com

20
FEB

Subaru Libero E12 Super Deluxe 4WD
vansofberlin.com

21
FEB

Volkswagen Type 2 / T3 Hightop Camper
vansofberlin.com

22
FEB

Mercedes-Benz O 309 Camper

vansofberlin.com

23
FEB

Volkswagen Type 2 / T2
vansofberlin.com

24
FEB

Mercedes-Benz 310 D Iglhaut 4WD Camper

vansofberlin.com

25

FEB

Volkswagen Type 2 / T3 Transporter
vansofberlin.com

26
FEB

Mercedes Benz 608 D Camper
vansofberlin.com

27
FEB

Peugeot J7 Camper
vansofberlin.com

28
FEB

Volkswagen Type 2 / T3 Joker Poptop Camper
vansofberlin.com

29
FEB

Schäfer Orion I Camper

1

MAR

Volkswagen Type 2 / T3 Transporter

vansofberlin.com

2
MAR

Ford Transit MK2 Camper
vansofberlin.com

3
MAR

Mercedes-Benz O 309 Camper

vansofberlin.com

4
MAR

Citroën C25 Alkoven Camper
vansofberlin.com

5
MAR

Volkswagen Type 2 / T3 Syncro Transporter
vansofberlin.com

6
MAR

Mercedes-Benz 508D Camper
vansofberlin.com

7
MAR

Volkswagen Type 2 / T3 Hightop Camper

vansofberlin.com

8

MAR

Mercedes-Benz Hymer-Mobil 540 Camper
vansofberlin.com

9
MAR

Mercedes-Benz 407 D Camper
vansofberlin.com

10
MAR

Volkswagen Type 2 / T3 Transporter Camper
vansofberlin.com

11
MAR

Mercedes-Benz 407 D Hightop Camper
vansofberlin.com

12
MAR

Mercedes-Benz 809 D Camper

vansofberlin.com

13
MAR

Volkswagen Type 2 / T3 Poptop Camper
vansofberlin.com

14
MAR

Mercedes-Benz 207 Alkoven Camper
vansofberlin.com

15
MAR

Volkswagen LT Hightop Camper

vansofberlin.com

16

MAR

Volkswagen Type 2 / T2
vansofberlin.com

17
MAR

Ford Transit MK1
vansofberlin.com

18
MAR

Bremach / Iveco 4WD Expedition Mobile
vansofberlin.com

19
MAR

Mercedes-Benz 309 D James Cook Hightop Camper
vansofberlin.com

20
MAR

Ford Falcon Motorhome

vansofberlin.com

21

MAR

Volkswagen Type 2 / T2 Hightop Camper
vansofberlin.com

22
MAR

Volkswagen Type 2 / T3 Hightop Camper
vansofberlin.com

23
MAR

Subaru Libero E12 Super Deluxe 4WD

vansofberlin.com

24

MAR

Iveco Daily 4WD Camper
vansofberlin.com

25
MAR

Volkswagen Type 2 / T3 Joker Hightop Camper
vansofberlin.com

26
MAR

Mercedes-Benz 407 D
vansofberlin.com

27
MAR

Opel Blitz LF8-TS
vansofberlin.com

28
MAR

Volkswagen Type 2 / T3 Hightop Camper
vansofberlin.com

29
MAR

Volkswagen Type 2 / T2
vansofberlin.com

30
MAR

Mercedes-Benz 508 D Camper
vansofberlin.com

31
MAR

Mercedes-Benz O 309 Camper

1

APR

Volkswagen Type 2 / T3 Poptop Camper
vansofberlin.com

2
APR

Mercedes-Benz 407 D Camper
vansofberlin.com

3
APR

Subaru Libero E12 Super Deluxe 4WD

vansofberlin.com

4

APR

Volkswagen Type 2 / T2
vansofberlin.com

5
APR

Volkswagen Type 2 / T3 Hightop Camper
vansofberlin.com

6
APR

Mercedes-Benz Unimog 406 4WD Expedition Truck
vansofberlin.com

7
APR

Mercedes-Benz 410 Camper
vansofberlin.com

8
APR

Renault S 170 TI 4WD Expedition Truck
vansofberlin.com

9
APR

Mercedes-Benz 208 Karmann Mobil Camper
vansofberlin.com

10
APR

Volkswagen Type 2 / T3 Hightop Camper
vansofberlin.com

11
APR

Volkswagen Type 2 / T3 Poptop Camper
vansofberlin.com

12
APR

Mercedes-Benz 210 D Camper
vansofberlin.com

13
APR

Volkswagen Type 2 / T3 Doka
vansofberlin.com

14
APR

Volkswagen LT Hightop Camper
vansofberlin.com

15
APR

Mercedes-Benz 608
vansofberlin.com

16
APR

Volkswagen Type 2 / T3 Karmann Mobil Gipsy Alkoven Camper
vansofberlin.com

17
APR

Volkswagen Type 2 / T3 Dehler Profi Hightop Camper
vansofberlin.com

18
APR

Mercedes-Benz 508 Camper
vansofberlin.com

19
APR

Mercedes-Benz 608 D Hightop Camper
vansofberlin.com

20
APR

Ford Transit MK2 Poptop Camper
vansofberlin.com

21
APR

Volkswagen Type 2 / T3 Transporter Camper
vansofberlin.com

22
APR

Büssing Konsul 11K Camper Bus
vansofberlin.com

23
APR

Mercedes-Benz 309 D Hymer Alkoven Camper
vansofberlin.com

24
APR

Volkswagen LT 28 D Hightop Camper
vansofberlin.com

25
APR

Mercedes-Benz Camper
vansofberlin.com

26
APR

Mercedes-Benz Camper
vansofberlin.com

27
APR

Subaru Libero E12 Super Deluxe 4WD
vansofberlin.com

28
APR

Mercedes-Benz 813 Camper Truck

vansofberlin.com

29

APR

Mercedes-Benz O 319 Panorama Camper Bus
vansofberlin.com

30
APR

Volkswagen Type 2 / T3 Transporter Syncro Camper

1
MAY

Volkswagen Type 2 / T2 Poptop Camper
vansofberlin.com

2
MAY

Mercedes-Benz Custom Alkoven Camper

vansofberlin.com

3
MAY

Volkswagen LT 35 Camper
vansofberlin.com

4
MAY

Volkswagen Type 2 / T3 Dehler Profi Hightop Camper
vansofberlin.com

5
MAY

Opel Blitz Camper
vansofberlin.com

6
MAY

Volkswagen Type 2 / T3 Transporter Camper

vansofberlin.com

7

MAY

Mercedes-Benz Arnold Camper
vansofberlin.com

8
MAY

Mercedes-Benz 308 Camper
vansofberlin.com

9
MAY

Mercedes-Benz 508 D Camper
vansofberlin.com

10
MAY

Ford Transit MK1 Hightop Camper
vansofberlin.com

11
MAY

Hanomag Henschel F45 Camper
vansofberlin.com

12
MAY

Volkswagen Type 2 / T3 Poptop Camper
vansofberlin.com

13
MAY

Volkswagen LT Hightop Camper
vansofberlin.com

14
MAY

DAF Langley Custom Camper
vansofberlin.com

15
MAY

Subaru Libero E12 Super Deluxe 4WD
vansofberlin.com

16
MAY

Volkswagen Type 2 / T1 Poptop Camper
vansofberlin.com

17
MAY

Volkswagen Type 2 / T3 Joker Poptop Camper
vansofberlin.com

18
MAY

Mercedes-Benz 207 Tabbert Condor 550 M Alkoven Camper
vansofberlin.com

19
MAY

Volkswagen Type 2 / T2 Camper
vansofberlin.com

20
MAY

Mercedes-Benz 508 D Camper
vansofberlin.com

21
MAY

Mercedes-Benz 508 Camper
vansofberlin.com

22
MAY

Volkswagen Type 2 / T3 Transporter Camper

vansofberlin.com

23
MAY

Subaru Libero E12 Super Deluxe 4WD

vansofberlin.com

24
MAY

Mercedes-Benz 813 Ice Truck

vansofberlin.com

25

MAY

Volkswagen Type 2 / T3 Transporter Camper

vansofberlin.com

26

MAY

Volkswagen Type 2 / T3 Hightop Camper
vansofberlin.com

27
MAY

Mercedes-Benz 207 Hightop Camper
vansofberlin.com

28
MAY

Volkswagen Type 2 / T2 Kemperink Camper
vansofberlin.com

29
MAY

Volkswagen Type 2 / T3 Hightop Camper
vansofberlin.com

30
MAY

Saurer 59 Bus

vansofberlin.com

31

MAY

Volkswagen Type 2 / T2 Poptop Camper

1

JUN

Ford Transit MK1
vansofberlin.com

2
JUN

Volkswagen Type 2 / T2 Hightop Camper
vansofberlin.com

3
JUN

Mercedes-Benz 100 D Hightop Camper
vansofberlin.com

4
JUN

Volkswagen Type 2 / T3 Joker Poptop Camper
vansofberlin.com

5
JUN

Piaggio Ape 50
vansofberlin.com

6
JUN

Chevrolet Fleetwood Tioga RV
vansofberlin.com

7
JUN

Volkswagen Type 2 / T3 Joker Hightop Camper
vansofberlin.com

8
JUN

Mercedes Benz 508 D Camper
vansofberlin.com

9
JUN

Volkswagen Type 2 / T3 Syncro Poptop Camper
vansofberlin.com

10
JUN

Volkswagen Type 2 / T2 Poptop Camper
vansofberlin.com

11
JUN

Mercedes-Benz 407 D Custom Camper
vansofberlin.com

12
JUN

Volkswagen Type 2 / T3 Hightop Camper
vansofberlin.com

13
JUN

Volkswagen Type 2 / T2 Hightop Camper
vansofberlin.com

14
JUN

Mercedes-Benz 306 D Poptop Camper
vansofberlin.com

15
JUN

Volkswagen Type 2 / T3 Poptop Camper

vansofberlin.com

16
JUN

Volkswagen LT Hightop Camper
vansofberlin.com

17
JUN

Mercedes-Benz Arnold Camper

vansofberlin.com

18
JUN

Mercedes-Benz 508 D Camper
vansofberlin.com

19
JUN

Mercedes-Benz 1017 Custom Camper Truck
vansofberlin.com

20
JUN

Opel (Bedford) Blitz Hymer-Mobil 521 Camper
vansofberlin.com

21
JUN

Mercedes-Benz 508 D Camper
vansofberlin.com

22
JUN

Hanomag Henschel F45 Camper
vansofberlin.com

23
JUN

Kässbohrer Setra S 150 Camper Bus
vansofberlin.com

24
JUN

Volkswagen Type 2 / T2 Hightop Camper
vansofberlin.com

25
JUN

Kässbohrer Setra S 6 Panorama Bus

vansofberlin.com

26

JUN

Mercedes-Benz 206 D Hightop Camper
vansofberlin.com

27
JUN

Volkswagen Type 2 / T3 Hightop Camper
vansofberlin.com

28
JUN

Volkswagen LT 28 D Hightop Camper
vansofberlin.com

29
JUN

Mitsubishi L300 Alkoven Camper
vansofberlin.com

30
JUN

Mercedes-Benz 813 Custom Camper Truck

1
JUL

Mercedes-Benz 207 D James Cook Hightop Camper

vansofberlin.com

2

JUL

Ford Transit MK2 Alkoven Camper
vansofberlin.com

3
JUL

Mercedes-Benz 407 D Camper
vansofberlin.com

4
JUL

Volkswagen LT Hightop Camper
vansofberlin.com

5
JUL

Volkswagen Type 2 / T3 Hightop Camper
vansofberlin.com

6
JUL

Mercedes-Benz Hymer-Mobil Camper
vansofberlin.com

7
JUL

Volkswagen LT AAC Sinus Hightop Camper
vansofberlin.com

8
JUL

Volkswagen Type 2 / T3 Transporter Camper
vansofberlin.com

9
JUL

Mercedes-Benz 508 D Camper
vansofberlin.com

10
JUL

Suzuki Carry Van

vansofberlin.com

11

JUL

Mercedes-Benz 508 D Camper
vansofberlin.com

12
JUL

Mercedes-Benz 813 Camper Truck

vansofberlin.com

13
JUL

Peugeot J7 Camper
vansofberlin.com

14
JUL

Volkswagen Type 2 / T3 Hightop Camper
vansofberlin.com

15
JUL

Ford Transit MK1
vansofberlin.com

16
JUL

Subaru Libero E12 Super Deluxe 4WD
vansofberlin.com

17
JUL

Volkswagen Type 2 / T3 Dehler Profi Hightop Camper

vansofberlin.com

18

JUL

Mercedes-Benz Hymer-Mobil S 560 Camper
vansofberlin.com

19
JUL

Volkswagen Type 2 / T3 Poptop Camper
vansofberlin.com

20
JUL

Volkswagen LT Hightop Camper

vansofberlin.com

21
JUL

Volkswagen Type 2 / T3 Syncro Hightop Camper

vansofberlin.com

22

JUL

Mercedes-Benz 608 D Hightop Camper

vansofberlin.com

23

JUL

Büssing Konsul 11K Camper Bus
vansofberlin.com

24
JUL

Mercedes-Benz Hymer-Mobil 540 Camper
vansofberlin.com

25
JUL

Mercedes-Benz 508 D Hightop Camper
vansofberlin.com

26
JUL

Mercedes-Benz 508 D Camper
vansofberlin.com

27
JUL

Mercedes-Benz Hymer-Mobil 700 Camper

vansofberlin.com

28
JUL

Ford Transit MK2 Pilote Camper
vansofberlin.com

29
JUL

Magirus Deutz 170 D 12 4WD Expedition Truck
vansofberlin.com

30
JUL

Volkswagen Type 2 / T2 Poptop Camper
vansofberlin.com

31
JUL

Mercedes-Benz Camper

1
AUG

Fiat 242 Ruggeri Tahiti Camper

vansofberlin.com

2

AUG

Volkswagen Type 2 / T3 Dehler Profi Hightop Camper

vansofberlin.com

3
AUG

Mercedes-Benz 207 D Camper
vansofberlin.com

4
AUG

Mercedes-Benz 508 D Camper
vansofberlin.com

5
AUG

Ford Transit MK2 Alkoven Camper
vansofberlin.com

6
AUG

Hanomag Henschel F20 Hightop Camper
vansofberlin.com

7
AUG

Steyr Puch Pinzgauer 6WD

vansofberlin.com

8
AUG

Volkswagen Type 2 / T2 Poptop Camper
vansofberlin.com

9
AUG

Volkswagen Type 2 / T3 Hightop Camper
vansofberlin.com

10
AUG

Volkswagen Type 2 / T2 Hightop Camper
vansofberlin.com

11
AUG

Renault Estafette

vansofberlin.com

12
AUG

Opel Bedford Blitz Poptop Camper

vansofberlin.com

13
AUG

Renault TRM 4000 4WD Expedition Truck
vansofberlin.com

14
AUG

Subaru Libero E12 Super Deluxe 4WD
vansofberlin.com

15
AUG

Volkswagen Type 2 / T3 Transporter Camper
vansofberlin.com

16
AUG

Mitsubishi L300 Alkoven Camper

vansofberlin.com

17
AUG

Mercedes-Benz 508 D Camper
vansofberlin.com

18
AUG

Kässbohrer Setra S 8 Panorama Bus

vansofberlin.com

19

AUG

Volkswagen Type 2 / T3 Syncro Hightop Camper
vansofberlin.com

20
AUG

Avia A30 Camper
vansofberlin.com

21
AUG

Mercedes-Benz 410 D Custom Camper
vansofberlin.com

22
AUG

Hanomag Henschel F45 Camper
vansofberlin.com

23
AUG

Volkswagen Type 2 / T3 Hightop Camper

vansofberlin.com

24
AUG

Volkswagen Type 2 / T3 Poptop Camper
vansofberlin.com

25
AUG

Volkswagen Type 2 / T2 Camper
vansofberlin.com

26
AUG

Mercedes-Benz O 3500 Camper Bus
vansofberlin.com

27
AUG

Mercedes-Benz 508 D Camper
vansofberlin.com

28
AUG

Mercedes-Benz 307 D Hightop Camper
vansofberlin.com

29
AUG

Volkswagen Type 2 / T3 Hightop Camper
vansofberlin.com

30
AUG

Barkas B 1000
vansofberlin.com

31
AUG

Heku Fiat Talento Camper

1
SEP

Volkswagen Type 2 / T3 Syncro Hightop Camper

vansofberlin.com

2
SEP

Mercedes-Benz 508 D Camper
vansofberlin.com

3
SEP

Volkswagen LT Hightop Camper
vansofberlin.com

4
SEP

Mercedes-Benz 407 D Camper
vansofberlin.com

5
SEP

Volkswagen Type 2 / T3 Poptop Camper
vansofberlin.com

6
SEP

Volkswagen Type 2 / T3 Hightop Camper
vansofberlin.com

7
SEP

Volkswagen Type 2 / T2 Camper
vansofberlin.com

8
SEP

Mercedes-Benz 608 D Camper

vansofberlin.com

9
SEP

Volkswagen LT 4WD
vansofberlin.com

10
SEP

Volkswagen Type 2 / T2 Poptop Camper
vansofberlin.com

11
SEP

Volkswagen Type 2 / T3 Hightop Camper
vansofberlin.com

12
SEP

Renault Estafette
vansofberlin.com

13
SEP

Volkswagen Type 2 / T3 Transporter Camper
vansofberlin.com

14
SEP

Mercedes-Benz 407 D Camper
vansofberlin.com

15
SEP

Volkswagen Type 2 / T3 Syncro Poptop Camper

vansofberlin.com

16
SEP

Kässbohrer Setra S 80 Custom Camper Bus
vansofberlin.com

17
SEP

Mercedes-Benz O 309 Camper

vansofberlin.com

18
SEP

Mercedes-Benz 508 D Camper
vansofberlin.com

19
SEP

Ford Transit MK1 Poptop Camper
vansofberlin.com

20
SEP

Volkswagen Type 2 / T3 Hightop Camper
vansofberlin.com

21
SEP

Hanomag Kurier
vansofberlin.com

22
SEP

Mercedes-Benz 608 D Hightop Camper
vansofberlin.com

23
SEP

Volkswagen Type 2 / T3 Poptop Camper
vansofberlin.com

24
SEP

Mercedes-Benz 406 D Camper
vansofberlin.com

25
SEP

Volkswagen Type 2 / T3 Transporter
vansofberlin.com

26
SEP

Ford E-Series
vansofberlin.com

27
SEP

Volkswagen Type 2 / T3 Poptop Camper
vansofberlin.com

28
SEP

Mercedes-Benz 508 D Alkoven Camper
vansofberlin.com

29
SEP

Volkswagen Type 2 / T3 Transporter Camper
vansofberlin.com

30
SEP

Peugeot D4A

1

OCT

Mercedes-Benz Hymer-Mobil Camper
vansofberlin.com

2
OCT

Mercedes-Benz Hymer-Mobil Camper
vansofberlin.com

3 OCT

Volkswagen LT Karmann Alkoven Camper
vansofberlin.com

4
OCT

Peougeot J7 Camper Van
vansofberlin.com

5
OCT

Ford Transit MK2
vansofberlin.com

6
OCT

Mercedes-Benz O 312 H-L Camper Bus
vansofberlin.com

7
OCT

Volkswagen Type 2 / T3 Doka
vansofberlin.com

8
OCT

Mercedes-Benz 207 D Hightop Camper
vansofberlin.com

9
OCT

Volkswagen Type 2 / T3 Hightop Camper
vansofberlin.com

10
OCT

Mercedes-Benz 309 D James Cook Hightop Camper

vansofberlin.com

11

OCT

Volvo C303 4WD Camper
vansofberlin.com

12
OCT

Mercedes-Benz 409 Camper
vansofberlin.com

13
OCT

Mercedes-Benz 406 D Alkoven Camper
vansofberlin.com

14
OCT

Volkswagen Type 2 / T3 Dehler Profi Hightop Camper

vansofberlin.com

15

OCT

Mercedes-Benz Hymer-Mobil 700 Camper
vansofberlin.com

16
OCT

Mercedes-Benz 508 D Camper
vansofberlin.com

17
OCT

Mercedes-Benz Hymer-Mobil Camper
vansofberlin.com

18
OCT

Volkswagen LT Sven Hedin Hightop Camper
vansofberlin.com

19
OCT

Volkswagen Type 2 / T2 Camper

vansofberlin.com

20
OCT

Volkswagen Type 2 / T3 Hightop Camper

vansofberlin.com

21

OCT

Ford Transit MK2 Camper
vansofberlin.com

22
OCT

Mercedes-Benz 308
vansofberlin.com

23
OCT

Mercedes-Benz 207 Alkoven Camper
vansofberlin.com

24
OCT

Volkswagen LT 28 D Hightop Camper
vansofberlin.com

25
OCT

Volkswagen Type 2 / T3 Hightop
vansofberlin.com

26
OCT

Volkswagen Type 2 / T3 Dehler Profi Hightop Camper

vansofberlin.com

27
OCT

Mercedes-Benz Hymer-Mobil Camper
vansofberlin.com

28
OCT

Volkswagen Type 2 / T3 Club Joker Hightop Camper
vansofberlin.com

29
OCT

Subaru Libero E12 Super Deluxe 4WD

vansofberlin.com

30
OCT

Mercedes-Benz 230 W110 Hearse

vansofberlin.com

31
OCT

Mercedes-Benz 508 D Expedition Camper

1
NOV

Opel (Bedford) Blitz Hymer-Mobil Camper
vansofberlin.com

2
NOV

Mercedes-Benz 508 D Camper
vansofberlin.com

3
NOV

Mitsubishi L300 Frankia Alkoven Camper
vansofberlin.com

4
NOV

Volkswagen Type 2 / T3 Transporter Camper

vansofberlin.com

5

NOV

Volkswagen Type 2 / T3 Joker Hightop Camper
vansofberlin.com

6
NOV

Opel (Bedford) Blitz Hymer Mobil 521 Camper
vansofberlin.com

7
NOV

Volkswagen Type 2 / T2 Camper
vansofberlin.com

8
NOV

Volkswagen Type 2 / T3 Poptop Camper
vansofberlin.com

9
NOV

Volkswagen Type 2 / T3 Transporter Camper

vansofberlin.com

10
NOV

Mitsubishi L300 Alkoven Camper
vansofberlin.com

11
NOV

Mercedes-Benz 407 D Camper

vansofberlin.com

12
NOV

Volkswagen Type 2 / T2 Camper
vansofberlin.com

13
NOV

Mercedes-Benz 508 D Alkoven Camper
vansofberlin.com

14
NOV

Volkswagen Type 2 / T2
vansofberlin.com

15
NOV

Peugeot J5 Custom Hightop Camper
vansofberlin.com

16
NOV

Volkswagen Type 2 / T2 Camper
vansofberlin.com

17
NOV

Subaru Libero E12 Super Deluxe 4WD

vansofberlin.com

18

NOV

Volkswagen Type 2 / T3 Dehler Profi Hightop Camper
vansofberlin.com

19
NOV

Mercedes-Benz 508 D Camper

vansofberlin.com

20

NOV

Volkswagen Type 2 / T2 Poptop Camper
vansofberlin.com

21
NOV

Volkswagen Type 2 / T3 Transporter Camper
vansofberlin.com

22
NOV

Mercedes-Benz 508 D
vansofberlin.com

23
NOV

Volkswagen LT Hightop Camper
vansofberlin.com

24
NOV

Mercedes-Benz 207 Arnold Camper
vansofberlin.com

25
NOV

Volkswagen Type 2 / T2 Camper
vansofberlin.com

26
NOV

Volkswagen Type 2 / T3 Transporter
vansofberlin.com

27
NOV

Mercedes-Benz 508 D Camper
vansofberlin.com

28
NOV

BLACK FRIDAY
Order any shop product
until **Dec, 2nd** and safe

15%

Your voucher code:

s+blck15

www.seltmannundsoehne.com
Worldwide shipping, free within Germany

Volkswagen LT Hightop Camper
vansofberlin.com

29
NOV

Peugeot Tabbert Camper
vansofberlin.com

30
NOV

MAN 415 DIESEL 4WD Expedition Mobile

1
DEC

Volkswagen Type 2 / T3 Hightop Camper
vansofberlin.com

2
DEC

Volkswagen Type 2 / T3 Poptop Camper
vansofberlin.com

3
DEC

Mercedes-Benz 308 Arnold Camper

vansofberlin.com

4

DEC

Volkswagen Type 2 / T3 Hightop Camper
vansofberlin.com

5
DEC

Mercedes-Benz 207 D James Cook Camper
vansofberlin.com

6
DEC

Volkswagen Type 2 / T3 Hightop Camper
vansofberlin.com

7
DEC

OUR X-MAS GIFT

Order your gifts for christmas online until **Dec, 10th** and safe

10%

Your voucher code:

s+xmas10

www.seltmannundsoehne.com

Worldwide shipping, free within Germany

Mercedes-Benz 710 4WD Expedition Truck
vansofberlin.com

8
DEC

Ford Transit MK2 Alkoven Camper
vansofberlin.com

9
DEC

Mercedes-Benz 710 4WD Expedition Truck
vansofberlin.com

10
DEC

Volkswagen Type 2 / T3 Poptop Camper
vansofberlin.com

11
DEC

Mercedes-Benz 407 D Hightop Camper

vansofberlin.com

12

DEC

Volkswagen Type 2 / T3 Poptop Camper

vansofberlin.com

13

DEC

Mercedes-Benz Unimog 1300 4WD Expedition Truck
vansofberlin.com

14
DEC

Volkswagen Type 2 / T3 Doka
vansofberlin.com

15
DEC

Mercedes-Benz 508 D Hightop Camper

vansofberlin.com

16

DEC

Mercedes-Benz 508 D
vansofberlin.com

17
DEC

Volkswagen LT Hightop Camper
vansofberlin.com

18
DEC

Mercedes-Benz 207 D Camper
vansofberlin.com

19
DEC

Steyr 680 4WD Expedition Truck

vansofberlin.com

20
DEC

Volkswagen Type 2 / T3 Poptop Camper
vansofberlin.com

21
DEC

Mercedes-Benz 310 D Hightop Camper
vansofberlin.com

22
DEC

Mercedes-Benz 207 D Hightop Camper

vansofberlin.com

23
DEC

Mercedes-Benz 310 D Iglhaut 4WD Camper

vansofberlin.com

24
DEC

Mercedes-Benz 508 D Camper
vansofberlin.com

25
DEC

Mercedes-Benz 508 D Camper
vansofberlin.com

26
DEC

Mercedes-Benz 508 D
vansofberlin.com

27
DEC

HAPPY NEW YEAR
Order our last calendars
until **Dec, 31st** and safe

10%

Your voucher code:

s+new10

www.seltmannundsoehne.com
Worldwide shipping, free within Germany

Volkswagen LT Hightop Camper
vansofberlin.com

28
DEC

Subaru Libero E12 Super Deluxe 4WD
vansofberlin.com

29
DEC

Mercedes-Benz 508 D Camper
vansofberlin.com

30
DEC

Magirus Deutz 170 D 11 4WD Expedition Truck
vansofberlin.com

31
DEC

The instagram page
@vansofberlin
is collecting vans, trucks and
camping vans in all variations
on the urban streets since 2014.

instagram.com/vansofberlin

IMPRINT

URBAN VANS

Publisher seltmann+söhne
Prinzenstraße 85D
10969 Berlin, Germany
www.seltmannundsoehne.com

Photographs © Linnart Unger
taken from the Instagram page @vansofberlin

Art Direction © Linnart Unger

Printed in Germany
Seltmann Printart, Lüdenscheid
www.seltmann.de

All type designations for the vans were
compiled carefully and to the best knowledge and certain.

All rigths reserved.
No part of this publication may be reproduced or transmitted
in any form or by any means, electronic or mechanical,
including photocopy, recording or any other storage and retrieval system,
without prior permission in writing from the publisher.

© 2018 seltmann+söhne

ISBN 978-3-946688-42-6